Newfoundland as Pets

The Ultimate Guide for Newfoundland Dogs General Info, Purchasing, Care, Cost, Keeping, Health, Supplies, Food, Breeding and More Included!

By Lolly Brown

Foreword

Newfoundland breed is known for being gentle giants as their sweetness is twice as big as their breed is. They get along well with humans and this breed love their presence especially of the children. They are a good loyal companion who is very affectionate and dignified. Of all these positive traits, these might not still be enough to determine whether owning one would best suit you and your family as well. So before you make a decision with regard to purchasing and taking care of a Newfoundland, you must first familiarize yourself with the characteristics of the breed you are about to deal with. All you need is enough time, effort, and of course, this book to do so.

Get ready as this book will discuss everything you need to know about the Newfoundland breed; from the history on how they came about down to the their most specific needs in terms of habitat, nutrition, grooming, health, and welfare. Enjoy!

Table of Contents

Introduction

Newfoundlands can look intimidating due to their size but they can be the sweetest and most gentle giant you'll ever see. They are known for being a friendly kind of breed. They also love working because dating back, they have been a great help in bringing ropes ashore, recovering fishing gears that have been lost, and rescuing humans in the wide seas of North Atlantic.

This breed is naturally smart and intelligent therefore they are fit for being trained. Generally, they are willing workers so expect that that most of them will enjoy training sessions. A very affectionate breed, they will surely love all the attention and care you will give them. They are very easy to socialize with as they are friendly in nature.

Having a dog is a long-term commitment. Before bringing a Newfoundland home make sure that you are emotionally, physically, mentally, and financially ready for you to be able to provide all the needs of your new pet. The well-being of your pet should always be your priority. It is your duty and responsibility to keep them healthy, safe, happy, and satisfied with the life they have. To make this possible, you must first be able to know all the necessary information about the dog you are about to deal with.

This book will help you gain knowledge on the general information, heritage, physical characteristics and temperament of Newfoundland dogs along with some guidelines on how to properly take care of this breed with regard to their health, grooming, habitat, maintenance, and nutrition. The standard of this breed will also be given as well how you'll be able to prepare yourself and your family for the newest member of the house. We are hoping that you'll be able to learn new things from this book whether you are a newbie or an experienced owner. We are very excited on how this book will turn out for you. Let the fun and learning start!

Chapter One: Basic Information

Sweetness of temperament is the hallmark of the Newfoundland as what the AKC Standard says. It is known to be a dignified, calm, and generally quiet dog. With all of these good qualities of this breed, it might not be enough to best suit others. Before you arrive into a conclusion whether or not this breed is for you, you must first familiarize yourself with the necessary information you need to know in order to see if a Newfoundland is the dog for you.

With the help of this chapter, you'll gain knowledge about the general information, biological facts along with the history of how it came about. This will help you depict if a Newfoundland breed is the perfect pet for you.

Taxonomy, Origin, and History

The Newfoundland has a scientific name of *Canis Familiaris*. They belong in Kingdom *Animalia*, Phylum *Chordata*, Class *Mammalia*, Order *Carnivora*, Family *Canidae*, Genus *Canis*, and Species *Lupus Familiaris*.

Newfoundland dogs also called as "Newfie" are said to originate in the island of Newfoundland in Canada and later they have been brought in England in the early 1800's. They came from both indigenous and black bear dogs that where introduced and brought by the Vikings. This breed is known as "ship dog "as they have been utilized in bringing ropes ashore, recovering fishing gears that have been lost and rescuing humans in the wide seas of North Atlantic. They have also been coined as a carting dog, sled dog and a pack animal

In the start of the fishing industry in the European continent, various breeds have somehow shaped and influenced the behaviour and characteristics of Newfoundlands but still their essential characteristics as being industrious and their features like being able to withstand the sea and the extreme climate has remained.

In the year 1775, an entrepreneur and a diarist in the person of George Cartwright named his dog with the name of his native island "Newfoundland."

It was the time that a first written record of the Newfoundland breed ever happened. During 1780, Richard Edwards the Commodore-Governor of Newfoundland limits the ownership of Newfoundlands legally in line of his promotion of sheep raising. An order of one dog per household has been strictly applied. Unfortunately, his drive towards sheep raising failed and the implementation of it actually led to the start of the extinction of native Newfoundland dogs. In this time, many dogs were exported and killed. Luckily, there are some who tried to break the law for the sake of their love for this breed that somehow helped the dogs survive in the island.

The 18th Century is the time wherein the Newfoundland dogs became popular and their number widely increased. In this era, the name of this breed has been used in different journals and other kinds of literature. Some of the artists and literary pieces on which the name of Newfoundlands appeared are Charlotte Bronte in Jane Eyre and in the Journals of the Lewis Clark Expedition to the Pacific Northwest written by Lewis Clark himself wherein he had his sea expeditions with a Newfoundland dog to accompany him.

Around the mid - nineteenth century, Sir Edwin Henry Landseer, a renowned English painter, has painted numbers of white and black Newfoundlands throughout his career. In his time, the white and black variety of this breed has been named "Landseer" after him.

In 1824, almost 2,000 of this breed are working in the city of St. John's Newfoundland, delivering haul loads as well as milk to the whole town. The ancestry of most of the Newfoundlands we have today are said to be related to an English Show Dog who lived in the 1920's.

Size, Life Span, and Physical Appearance

This breed has a massive and powerful body structure. Their body is compact and their robust muscles are well coordinated with all their movements and can withstand sea turbulent without drowning. Their body length is longer than their height and they have powerful gait along with a good drive.

Newfoundland coats are black in general but they can also be grey or brown and may also have some white markings as their coloration. Its soft and dense undercoat keeps them dry at the skin and warm. Their outer coat is medium in length and is water resistant.

A male Newfoundland stands 26 to 28 inches and has a general weight of 130 to 150 pounds. On the other hand, females stand in an average of 26 inches tall and weigh 100 up to 120 pounds. A Newfoundland female's body may be less massive and slightly longer compared to a male's. This breed can live up to 8 to 10 years of age in average. But there are cases wherein some of them reached 15 years of age.

Quick Facts

Origin: Newfoundland, Canada
Breed Size: large size breed
Body Type and Appearance: It has a massive and powerful body structure.
Group: Newfoundland Club of America, The Kennel Club, Welsh Newfoundland Activity Group, Northern Newfoundland Club
Height: a male Newfoundland stand 26 to 28 inches and females stand in an average of 26 inches tall

Weight: male has a general weight of 130 to 150 pounds; 100 to 120 pounds for females

Coat Length: long and straight without curl

Coat Texture: soft and dense

Color: Black, black and white, brown, gray and may come with white markings

Temperament: sweet, joyful, dignified and gentle

Strangers: they can easily get along with other people as they are naturally amiable and friendly towards humans.

Other Dogs: they can socialize well with other dogs especially if they are exposed at a very young age.

Other Pets: can get along with other pets but some are predatory towards cats.

Training: they are intelligent and are easy to train

Exercise Needs: daily walks, run in the yard, and casual swimming.

Health Conditions: generally healthy but are prone to common health problems including hip dysplasia, bloat, panosteitis, elbow dysplasia, cataracts, hyperthyroidism, aortic stenosis, pulmonic stenosis

Lifespan: average of 8 to 10 years

Other name: Newfie, Newf

Chapter Two: Getting to Know Newfoundland

After gaining knowledge on all the basic information about Newfoundland, we hope that you're now gaining insight about this hardworking and gentle breed but it doesn't stop there. It is only just the beginning! Before you make a decision if Newfoundland is the breed for you, there is still many things for you to discover.

With the aid of this chapter, you will be able to delve more vital information you need to know in order to make sure that this pet is ideal for you. We'll discuss how Newfoundland acts as a pet, how they deal with other animals, their temperament, and a compatibility check to see if you can handle such breed along with the requirements needed in order to keep one legally.

How does a Newfoundland Behave?

Being able to build a good and healthy relationship with your pet is something special and necessary. You have to invest your time, effort, love, and care to your dog in order for him to be affectionate to you as well. Having a dog is like choosing a partner in life. It's a long term emotional and financial commitment, therefore, you have to be really sure that you are ready to spend the rest of your time with the perfect pet for you. Having said that, you must make sure that your characteristics and personality match well with those of a Newfoundland in order for you to enjoy each other's company and that you are financially capable of providing what it needs.

To help you decide whether this kind of dog is for you, this segment will give you points about the personality of Newfoundlands in general, the cost of having one as a pet, together with some tips on how you can introduce and socialize them with other pets and see to it if you'll be able to get along with them based on their temperament and if your budget is fit for their needs.

Temperament and Behavioral Characteristics

- They are known for their gentleness and calmness.
- They are sweet tempered that's why they are called the "sweet giant"
- They are very devoted, loyal and affectionate to their owners.
- They can be protective whenever there is a need to.
- They make a good safeguard. If ever an intruder comes into your house, this breed will surely put the bad guy under arrest.
- They love attention from their owner and from other people.
- They are active and enjoy activities especially swimming.
- They are a great companion for hiking.
- They are very sociable and friendly even to others.
- They tend to suffer from "separation anxiety "whenever left alone therefore is in need of proper attention.
- They may exhibit a "destructive behaviour" when they become anxious.
- They may characterize excessive jumping especially if they are still a puppy.

- They are excellent with children as they have the patient when kids try to snuggle and play with them just like a natural babysitter.

Behavioral Characteristics with other Pets

- In general, they get along easily with dogs of any size especially if they have been socialized early and often.
- Some male dogs might be aggressive with other male dogs.
- Very few may act dominant toward other pets.

Compatibility Check

We have here for you a special segment you can make use of in order to determine if this breed is the ideal dog for you. If you can deal with the situations we'll present to you it means that you and a Newfoundland are a perfect fit for each other. Let the compatibility check begins!

Can you deal with…
- A quiet and dignified breed of dog?
- Their slobbering and drooling?
- Their heavy shedding?
- A thick coated and powerful pet?
- A playful and well-mannered house companion?

- A big dog that may take a lot of space both in your car and house?
- Making them a hiking companion?
- A dog who loves being around children?
- Having the need to spend time for their daily walk and exercise?
- Providing them proper socializing with other people and animals?
- Some problems about stubbornness?
- Having enough patience whenever they become dominant especially males?
- The need of providing them enough attention?
- Giving them your constant company as it is what their behavior demands and for them to avoid having a separation anxiety?
- Rendering them medical care if ever they catch illness?

If you can handle all or most of these situations, it means that you have the capacity to take care of a Newfoundland. It indicates that you are ready to accept both their positive and negative characteristics.

Legal Requirements and Dog Licensing

Traveling, who doesn't love that? Visiting places you've never been into, exploring new sceneries, and knowing the culture of different places have always been a wonderful thing to experience. But of course you wouldn't want to leave your pet alone at home right?

In some countries, there are some regulations and restrictions that you must be mindful of. If you are planning to bring your loving pet with you, there is a need for you to comply with all the requirements needed in order to avoid problems in your trip. However, other countries do not require licensing for dogs. But despite of this fact, you may still want to opt for such as it will protect your dog if ever it gets lost as there are licensing devices that can heighten your dog's safety.

Dog Licensing

United States

National requirements for dog licensing are not regulated in the United States. However, in the local level, there may be a need for your pet dog to be licensed. Most states and municipalities require dog owners to register and license their dogs. Documents such as current rabies vaccination certificate must be presented in the licensing office. Some states may require additional requirements before they release the permanent license. In the meantime, they will release a temporary one until you have complied with all the needed papers. Usually, dog licenses only cost about $25 annually as you renew the license along with the rabies vaccination.

United Kingdom

In the United Kingdom, unless the dog is six months or younger, a police dog, an assistance dog accompanying a person with disability, it's under a block license, or if it's intended to be sold in a licensed store, the owner needs to register and have their pet dog licensed individually. Dog licensing in the United Kingdom costs £12.50 and lasts for 12 months. You may apply to your council offices or you can find a dog license application form and dog license renewal form over your local council's website.

If ever you have more than 2 dogs, it will be more practical for you to apply for a group licensing called "block license" which costs £32. This type of license is as applicable as long as these two requirements are met (1) there are at least three unsterilized bitches breeding less than three litters over a year. (2) at least three dogs are registered guard dog kennels of the Irish Coursing Club, Masters of Foxhounds Association, Masters of Harriers and Beagles Association,International Sheep Dog Society, Northern Ireland Masters of Hounds Association, and Kennel Club.

Russia

When entering Russia, your pet must come from a place free from rabies for at least six months and the following requirements should be met. Your pet needs to be microchipped, a device implanted under your dog's skin. You must be able to present a vaccination certificate against rabies 21 days to 12 months prior the day you are entering to Russia. They should also be given shots for distemper, viral enteritis, parvovirus, adenovirus, and hepatitis. You must have a licensed veterinarian accomplish a Veterinary Certificate for Russia in the span of 5 days of travel assuring that the animal is healthy and have already been vaccinated against rabies.

Other Countries

In other countries, usually they require papers such as vaccination certificates, the state license of your dog, and other papers reflecting the health condition of your dog.

Importance of Dog Licensing

Whether or not the state or country you belong requires dog licensing, we still encourage you to register your pet as it can heighten your dog's safety making this process a very important one. After licensing, you'll be given a dog number. This number is linked to the owner's contact information. If by chance your dog got lost and someone with a good heart found him, he may use the information in the ID found in the collar of your pet.

Cost of Owning a Dog

In this segment, an overview of the costs related with the purchasing and other on-going cost of care will be given as you must be able to cover all these expenses for your dog. The cots you will encounter are namely the purchase price, accessories, toys,shelter, vaccinations, licensing/ micro-chipping, grooming supplies, and as well as spay/neuter surgery.

Are You Financially Prepared?

Taking care of dogs can be expensive regardless of the level on how it should be maintained. You have to provide for them the necessary supplies they need in order to be satisfied and be able to live a healthy and a happy life. If you are going to have a dog as your pet, make sure that your financial status is stable and you have enough money to provide everything your dog needs.

The costs of all the dog-related expenses depend on the store where you bought the supplies, the quality of the product, the brand of the item, the time being/season, etc. This part will help you verify if you are really financially prepared to have a Newfoundland as your pet.

Purchase Price of Newfoundland

Cost: $800 to $1500

The cost of Newfoundland depends on where you bought it. You may expect the amount of $800 to $1500 for a puppy being sold by a reputable breeder, in general. It is better for you to spend a huge amount of money in the start given that you are sure that the dog is well-raised as for the reason that it came from a highly-regarded breeder rather than buy a cheaper one from an irresponsible breeder as the puppy may be suffering from behavioural problems and infections that may lead to a bigger expense in the future.

Recurring Expenses

Expense doesn't stop in the purchase price for there are still recurring expenses you have to cover. There is still the need to buy supplementary things like food supplies, dishes, comfortable beds, grooming supplies, and dietary supplements. There is also a need for you to prepare money for the vaccinations as these are essential especially for puppies. You also have to consider other costs like micro-chipping, vet consultations, spay/neuter procedures, and other accessories.

Food and Healthy Treats

Cost: $480 to $800

You should be meticulous when it comes to the food you let your dog eat. You should provide them with nothing but of high-quality food and treats. It may look expensive but the nutrients it contains can give your dog protection from any illness and it will save you bucks from any medication and hospitalization. Newfoundland are huge dogs and their dietary needs are different from other regular-sized dogs. Expect that you will spend quite a lot of money when it comes to food. The cost of this ranges from $480 to 950 per annum.

Food Dishes and Water Bowl

Cost: $5 to $35

Stainless steel is what your dog dish/bowl should made of since this material is heavy duty, easier to clean, and less prone from bacteria accumulation. Steel bowls that of low quality can be bought for $5 dollars while a quality set of dish can be bought for $35

Bed

Cost: $50 to $250

Newfoundlands are large sized dogs, which mean that their bed might be more expensive than of the other dogs. It is advisable for you to buy a larger bed so that when the puppy grows up there is no need for you to buy another one. What an economical way to save money isn't? The average price of a dog bed that may suit your Newfoundland ranges from $50 to $250.

Toys

Cost: $25 to $200

The list of toys for a Newfoundland breed is far too long. You can choose any toy as long it's not too small for him to swallow. It should also be made from a high-quality material that won't break apart easily. There may be a need for you to buy toys more often as the dog outgrows the old one. Toys may cost $25 to $200 per year.

Grooming tools

Cost: $50- to $500

It is recommended for you to buy a good quality of grooming tools as these last longer than those of the low quality ones. You need a pin brush, nail clipper, shampoo, conditioner, towels, fine tooth comb, dog dryer, ear cleaning supplies, toothpaste, toothbrush, etc. grooming tools costs $50 to $500.

Leash and Collars

Cost: $25- $60

The cost for these accessories varies on the size and material they are made of. It is better to invest on a high-quality one. This may cost $25 to $60.

Medical Expenses

Cost: $50- $800

Medical expenses such as vaccinations, micro-chipping, spay/neuter surgery, and consultations to the vet should also be included in your budget as it is for the health and welfare of your dog

Micro-chipping

Cost: $30 to $50

It is a process of implanting a microchip bearing the owner's contact information under the dog's skin. By this process, if ever your dog will be lost by any means, the one who will find your dog shall bring your pet on the nearest shelter. They'll be able to track you down and help you be reunited with your pet within just a scan. The price for this procedure varies as it depends on where it was done but generally it costs $30 to $50.

Initial Vaccination

Cost: $50 above

Vaccinations are very essential in keeping the health condition of your dog exceptional. Besides from initial vaccinations, there are boosters needed to be shot in order to ensure their protection against any diseases. Make sure you consult your veterinarian about these and see to it that your pet will receive the needed vaccinations as soon as possible. This may cost $50 above depending on what your vet requires and prescribes.

Spay/Neuter Surgery

Cost: spay surgery $100 to $200/ neuter surgery $50 to $100

This procedure is done surgically. It is the process of extracting the testicles of a male dog and removing the ovaries and uterus of the female. In this way, you may prevent any unwanted pregnancies. It is advisable that this process be performed before the dog turn 6 months in able to provide the maximum protection against any reproductive order diseases. A neuter surgery costs $50 to $100 and spays surgery costs about $100 to $200 but this may vary on where the procedure has been done.

Veterinary Consultations

Cost: $200-$500

It is recommended to plan a visit to the vet at least twice a year in order to make sure that your dog is healthy and free from any potential infections.

Chapter Three: Purchasing a Healthy Breed from a Reputable Breeder

Choosing the dog you're going to spend most of your time with is a magical moment for all of the aspiring pet owners. Therefore you must really pay attention to all the factors you have to consider and one of it is the place and to whom you can acquire a healthy Newfoundland breed. The way the puppy has been raised is a vital part on the attitude and behaviour of the dog itself, having said that, one should really be meticulous on choosing a reputable breeder.

In this chapter, we'll help you hand in hand in selecting a Newfoundland breed and to whom or where you can purchase one. Let the road to choosing begin!

Where can I acquire a Newfoundland?

The place where you can find and purchase a good Newfoundland breed can be quite confusing as there are lots of places to choose from but you should always look after a reputable place as the environment where the dog has been raised or where it stayed can greatly affect its behaviour.

Local Pet Stores

A pet store is the first place that you might consider in buying a dog as it is the most common place to do so.

Pros

- It's the most convenient place to look for a pet as there are lots of pet stores located in the busy streets of your town.
- It is where you can find a purebred kind of dog.
- The dog you will acquire from a pet store is in a good health condition as to their store quality.
- The dogs here usually have a proper and complete documentation.

- The price you will pay is less expensive than on the other sellers.

Cons

- Pet stores are considered by some breeders as a "bad industry" since they claim that pet stores aren't taking care of pets as their own but they keep them for the mere purpose of business only. As they have sold and emptied one cage they will restock dogs which are very alarming for their welfare.
- The behaviour of the dog you might acquire in a pet store can be problematic as the dogs here have been separated from their parent at a very young age.
- A dog that was raised inside a cage can be hyperactive therefore dogs here have a tendency to be barking excessively.
- The dogs in a pet store are said to be coming from a puppy mill, a place where puppies are raised and kept in a not so nice environment and condition, making them more sickly and prone to infection.

Private Breeders

This kind of breeder can be associated with those who raise their dogs personally. They can be considered as the first owner of the puppies.

Pros

- They are the ones who personally know the behavior of the dog you are about to acquire. Having said that, you may ask for some pointers on how to deal with your new pet.
- Private breeders are the ones taking care of the puppies personally therefore you'll be able to see if they are reputable or not depending on how the puppies were raised.
- The price each puppies are sold can still be negotiated depending on what amount best fits your budget.

Cons

- For you to be able to buy a dog from a private breeder, you must visit their location which can be inconvenient for you if you are living far from their place.

- You have to personally pick up the dog you chose which can cost you transportation expenses

Online Stores

The internet has really helped us with regard to making our life convenient. Within just one click you'll be able to find the pet of your choice.

Pros

- You'll be able to choose a dog beforehand without the need to travel all the way to their location
- Advertisements are circulating around the world wide web of different pet websites where you can purchase a dog which will help you save time and effort.
- Usually, there is a review section in each website that will give you an insight on the reputation of the online store you visited.

Cons

- There is a need for you to visit the location of the breeder you have chosen for you to be sure that the dogs are well-raised.

- If ever you came drove a long way and found out that the dogs aren't well raised, it can a big waste of time.
- There are some advertisements bearing false information about the online store. The pictures they are using might not be the actual condition of the pets they sell.
- There are stores that have been made for scamming and are really non-existent which can be really alarming.

Dog Conventions

These are events held for all the dog lovers and aspiring pet owners. These can be an annual event you will surely enjoy.

Pros

- You'll be able to meet lots of dog breeders and pet owners and you can ask for their experiences and you can share yours too.
- This kind of event is full of breeders of high repute and dog enthusiasts. Being surrounded with these kinds of people can really bring out the dog lover in you.
- The quality of dogs here is highly regarded.

- Vaccination papers and/or proper licensing requirements of the dog you acquire are usually provided.

Cons

- These conventions are usually crowded with a large traffic of aspiring pet owners.
- There is a tendency that you'll have to wait for months for the next event as these aren't a daily thing which can be a problem if you want to have a dog right at the moment.

Steps in Finding a Reputable Breeder

The question who to buy a dog from is another question we'll answer for you. Finding a highly regarded breeder is essential as it mirrors the characteristics instilled upon the dogs it raise. If the breeder is responsible and caring, then you can be sure that the dogs he breed are raised in a a good and healthy environment.

Investigate

It's time for you to unveil your inner Sherlock. In order for you to be sure that you are dealing with the right breeder you can ask for referrals from other dog owners or you can inquire in pet stores, groomers, and veterinary offices for Newfoundland breeders. To further investigate, you should check out the website for each breeder if ever they have one in order for you to see the their experience in taking care of the breed of your choice, their registration in national or to which local breed club they belong, and other vital information. If ever the website looks suspicious and lacks information, do not waste your time and move on to another breeder on your list.

Interview

Contact the breeder and conduct a small interview. You can ask about their whole experience in taking care of a Newfoundland. Through this you can measure their knowledge about this breed. You can ask for information about the dog's registration number, and health background, and even the breeding stock including the breeding program they use. Verify if the breeder offers health guarantees and inquire about any vaccinations the puppies/dogs may already have. One sign that the breeder you are having a conversation with is accountable if he asks questions about yourself too. It means that they are making sure that the dog or dogs he own will be transferred in good hands and will be well-taken care of.

Inspect

You may request for an ocular visit on the facilities of the breeder you chose for you to verify if they are accommodating the dogs well. Inspect the area where the dogs have been raised and if ever it is not in a good condition, you may opt to see another breeder.

What Should I Consider in Choosing a Newfoundland

If you have already decided that a Newfoundland is the best breed for you, it's now time to choose one. Choosing a dog must not be done impulsively but rather you have to make some considerations. You need to pay close attention to all the details no matter how big or small they are. In choosing the pet you're going to invest your time and love with, you must make sure that they are in a good and healthy condition, and their temperament/behaviour is exceptional. We have here for you some parameters you may consider in choosing the right dog to acquire.

Physical Appearance

Physical appearance is the most obvious thing you'll notice. Therefore you must examine carefully the dog you're about to purchase. Observe if the dog is active and free from any infection. Look for any signs of body abnormality, illness and potential injuries. Check the coat color and texture. See to it that it has a healthy coat and free from any parasites. Make sure that the dog's eyes and ears, as well as the nasal passage, are free from discharge or inflammation. Check for the teeth and gums if it's healthy and in a good pinkish condition.

Temperament

The temperament or behaviour is the thing that will connect you to your pet dog. If both of your characteristics jive well, you'll be able to live together happily. For you to be able to determine the behavior of the puppy, observe how they interact with other dogs inside a litter box. Try to play with them, pet and call them over to see if they can go socialize and get along with humans. Pick them up and hold them, if they immediately shy away it means that they are not properly socialized by the breeder. Make sure that the puppy you will choose is not overly shy but is should be friendly and lets you handle them. Look if there are signs of excessive barking as it indicates that the dog is hyperactive.

List of Breeders and Rescue Websites

For you to be able to choose a reputable breeder, we have here a list of websites you may want to consider in order to acquire a Newfoundland from a breeder of high repute.

We also included a list of rescue websites where you can adopt a Newfoundland. There are a number of dogs being maltreated and abandoned by their owners looking for a new home to stay and a new family to live with. They are knocking at your hearts, maybe you're the one destined to help them erase all the bad things they went through and start over with new joyful memories. Remember that adopting a dog is like saving a life and bringing a new hope.

United States Breeders and Rescue Websites

Manitouloa Newfoundlands
<http://www.manitouloanewfoundlands.com/>

TidesPointe Newfoundlands
<http://www.tidespointenewfoundlands.com/>

Beach Bear Newfoundlands
<https://beachbearnewfoundlands.com/>

Sandy Cove Newfoundlands
<http://www.sandycovenewfs.com/>

Capricorn Newfoundlands
<https://capricornnewfoundlands.com/>

Alii Shores Newfoundlands
<http://www.newfs.com/>

Denali Farm Newfoundlands
<http://www.denalinewf.com/>

Ebb Tide
<http://www.ebbtidekennels.com/>

Pandaga Newfoundlands
<http://www.pandaganewfs.com/>

Newf Rescue
<http://www.newfrescue.com/>

Newfoundland Club of America
<http://www.ncarescue.org/>

Colonial Newfoundland Rescue
<http://www.colonialnewfrescue.org/>

South Central Newfoundland Rescue
<http://www.scnewfrescue.org/>

United Kingdom Breeders and Rescue Websites

The Kennel Club
< www.thekennelclub.org.uk/>

Newfoundland Puppy Breeders
<http://newfoundlandpuppybreeders.uk/>

Champdogs
<https://www.champdogs.co.uk/breeds/newfoundland/breeders?start=all/>

The Newfoundland Club
<http://www.thenewfoundlandclub.co.uk/>

Sandbears Newfoundland
<http://sandbears.com/>

The Inkomo Stud
<http://www.inkomostud.co.uk/>

Southern Newfoundland Club
<http://www.inkomostud.co.uk/>

Barachois
<https://www.barachois.co.uk/>

Darkpeak Newfoundlands

<http://www.darkpeaknewfoundlands.co.uk/#!/pageSplash>

Northern Newfoundland Club

<http://www.northernnewfoundlandclub.org.uk/welfare.ht
ml/>

UK Newfoundland Rescue

<http://newfoundland.rescueme.org/uk>

Chapter Four: Preparing a Home for Newfoundland

The place where your Newfoundland dwells is a vital factor in its well-being. The environment it lives in plays a significant role on its mood, behaviour, and health condition. For you to ensure that your pet is happy and satisfied with its new home, you have to make extreme measures in making your house a Newfoundland-friendly one. You'll learn, in this chapter, ways on how to make your house the best home for your dog. We'll give you a list of the things your pet needs from its shelter down to other essential accessories and some preparations you need to do before the arrival of the newest member of your family.

Housing Requirements

Comfort is the main factor you should consider in providing a good home for your Newfoundlands. Every dog needs a place to call their own and therefore you must respect their territory and space. This breed is a large one and is need of a spacious place to stay and rest.

Dog Bed

Usually, Newfoundlands prefer to lie down on a cool floor but others still appreciate the cushioning of a comfy bed. It is advisable for you to buy a bigger bed since it will be more practical. As the puppy grows up, there will be no need for you to buy a new bed, unless it has already been worn out, making you save bucks. Make sure that the material it is made of are of the highest quality to ensure that it will last long.

Important Note:

If ever your dog doesn't sleep on the bed you bought do not force them to do so as it may cause them stress. Let them first adjust on its new environment. Do not be too pushy. Remember that your dog's comfort should be your priority and if he chooses to stay in the floor let him

Tip:

Do not lose hope that your dog might just ignore the bed you have set. In order to encourage him, you can try to put his favourite treats on the bed luring him to stay on it. Give him praises and compliments if he stayed in the bed.

Cage

Many advocates say that making your dog stay in a cage is somehow abusive as it limits and robs their freedom. Newfoundlands are very affectionate and is always in need of a companion. Making them live in a cage alone might cause them the development of "separation anxiety," a disorder that makes the dog anxious and depressed. It is not advisable for you to let your dog stay in a confined area but rather let them roam around and feel that they belong and that they can do whatever they want and be wherever they want, but still under your supervision of course.

Important Note:

You may still opt on buying a cage so that if ever you travel, you may bring your dog with you. You should be very careful in buying a cage. Make sure that it will only look like a cozy den rather than a confining one so that your dog will not be intimidated and they will not feel like they have been imprisoned.

Play Pen

Playing is something Newfoundlands enjoy. You must ensure that your dog gets sufficient time in playing. This activity can actually improve both the physical and mental development of your pet. Plus, it can be a good way to bond with them. You may want to provide them a play pen in order to keep them safe and protected especially if you're going to let them play in the yard. A decent place to play will surely be appreciated by your dog.

Toys

To further intensify his enjoyment during playtime, you may want to find toys appropriate for him. You may actually buy any kind of toy as long as it is not too small for them to swallow. Buy toys that are ultra-durable so that there will be no need for you to buy a new toy every now and then. Newfoundlands need distraction from boredom. Showering them with toys can help them beat idle time.

Housing Temperature

Heat and Newfoundlands doesn't go well together. This breed has a heavy thick coat and they cannot deal well in a hot weather or temperature. It should be kept in a cold to temperate weather. If it is summer time it is recommended that you let your dog indoors as much as possible as they may catch heat stroke easily. You may have the need to provide your dog air coolers or electric fans whenever the weather is too hot for them.

Preparations before the Arrival of Your Dog

Brief the whole family

If you are living with your family, let them know that a new addition to the house is coming. Make sure that everyone wholeheartedly commits in welcoming the newest member of the family. You can try to assign who's going to feed, who's going to walk the dog in the morning, and any other tasks needed to be accomplished daily. Remember that having a dog is a family affair.

Buy essential supplies

Buy the needed things ahead of time so that when your dog arrives everything will be set. Go and shop for food and water bowls, bed, treats, leash, collar, toys, grooming supplies, etc.

Prepare your house

This requires effort and time. Make sure that the new home of your dog is puppy proof. In this way, your dog will be kept safe and away from any accidents and from the things that might harm them. Below are the steps on how to properly dog proof your home.

- Keep them out of reach from toxic plants like azalea and calla lily. If you own these kinds of plants, get rid of them immediately.
- Keep chemicals and any other cleaning supplies like bleach, fabric softener, and acids on the topmost shelf to prevent chemical intoxication
- Electric cords are very dangerous for your dog as they have the tendency to chew them. Make sure that you are able to tie up loose cords and keep them away from it as much as possible.
- See to it that the doors and windows are properly closed to prevent escaping and falling.
- Store away food that may intoxicate your pet like onion, chocolate, coffee, tea, grapes, nuts and the likes.
- Keep away tobacco products as they can be fatal for your dog.
- Put away sharp objects like knives from your dog's reach.

- Secure gasoline oil, fertilizers, and insecticides inside sealed containers.
- Keep all garbage inside closed bins.
- Set up a screen protecting your dog from the fireplace as they may get hurt from the flames or ashes.
- Install fences in your yard to prevent your dog from slipping out.
- Keep away vulnerable items as they might be knocked over by your dog.
- Close staircase with a baby gate.
- Pools and ponds should be enclosed with fences to prevent your pet from drowning.
- Have air coolers and electric fans in your home in case the temperature rises.
- Put away scraps like chicken bones, meat trimmings, coffee grounds, and food wraps.
- Keep small things away that might be easily swallowed by your dog like jewelries, coins, clips, and needle .
- Make sure that your pet won't have any access on the parts of your house that might be dangerous for them like the bathroom and kitchen.,
- Install latches and child locks on the cabinets.
- Keep socks, nylon, and underwear off the floor.

Arrange your trip home

Puppies might be afraid and shaking on the day you pick them up. You may ask for someone to assist you in doing so or you may use a crate in bringing them home alone. Make the trip comfortable for your dog. You can pet them and give them treats to help them relax.

Chapter Five: Diet and Nutrition

You are what you eat, as they say. This saying goes for dogs as well; if they'll be able to intake nutritious and high-quality food, their health will surely be in the best state. Nutrition is something an owner must really focus on as it is where the energy and health of your dog relies on. This is not something that should be compromised. Nutritional and dietary needs of dogs differ. It greatly depends on factors like weight, age, and their level of activity within the day. It is a must that you'll be able to provide them the correct nutrition they need, nothing more nothing less.

In this chapter, we'll help you learn tips on how to feed your dog properly and how you'll be able to give them the best nutrition. There will be a list of food that can potentially harm your dog that you may have to avoid. Brands of dog food, along with its ratings and reviews, will also be provided

FAQS

How many calories does a Newfoundland need?

Based on the National Research Council of the National Academies, a 130-pound active Newfoundland is in need of an average daily intake of 2695kcal. For those dogs that underwent spaying and neutering, they may need a fewer amount of calories

Puppies consume more number of calories than of the adult dogs as their metabolism differs. Young Newfoundland with the weight of 88 pounds and 6 months old requires 2227kcal per day. Remember that their calorie needs depends on the size and the level of activity they have. There is a need for you to adjust their food intake if the situation demands.

What vitamins and minerals are prescribed for Newfoundlands?

You must feed your dog with food that are properly formulated and packed with the nutrients they need. Below are some nutrient requirements for you Newfoundlands.

- **Taurine** - This prevents certain heart diseases and regulates proper muscle functions. It is also a great antioxidant. This breed has a higher chance of developing taurine deficiency that might cause serious health risks like dilated cardiomyopathy, a common heart disease associated with large dogs like this breed.

- **Arginine** - this amino acid keeps dogs active, healthy, and away from heart diseases and cancer.

- **Iodine** - This is necessary to regulate the growth and rate of your dog's metabolism. Iodine deficiency is the cause of hyperthyroidism which causes poor growth and behavioural changes.

- **Omega 3 and Omega 6** - Dogs need fat for their healthy diet but these fats are healthy fats of course. Omegas are found to lower blood cholesterol and lower risk of cancer.

- **Calcium and Phosphorous** - These two are vital in keeping bones and muscles strong which is very essential for large breeds.

How frequent should I feed my dog?

The frequency on how often you should feed your dog relies on its size, age, weight, and activity level. If your dog is more active, it requires more energy from food. It is advisable that your dog intakes the amount of food 2-3% of its body weight per day.

According to the Newfoundland Club of America, puppies whose age range between 3 months and 18 months, eat a lot as they are preparing themselves for growth but when they reach the age of maturity, they tend to eat less. The club requires that a puppy should eat 3 meals per day while a 5-6 months dog can eat 2 meals per day. The change in your dog's diet should be made gradually for his body to adjust properly. Be careful not to overfeed your pet as an overweight dog is more prone on getting sick and catching disorders like elbow and hip dysplasia.

What should I do if my dog refuses to eat?

Do not force your dog to eat if ever he refuses. Leave the food on his reach and eventually when he gets hungry he'll try to eat the food you've served. You can try to change the dog food you offer as they may become picky. Taking your dog for a walk before mealtime can help increase his appetite.

When should I feed my dog?

It is recommended for you to establish a schedule on the time you are going to feed your dog probably in the morning and in the evening. By this way, your dog will know when to expect his meal.

How often should I give treats?

Treats should only take up 5% of the total daily calorie needs of your dog. Limit giving out treats as it may cause obesity.

What type of dog food should I let my pet eat?

Foods that are rich in protein, fibre, and carbohydrates should be the kind of food you let your dog have. Buy products that are stamped by the Association of American Feed Control Officials (AAFCO) as they have been approved safe by the officials. You may ask your veterinarian for recommendations.

Types of Standard Commercial Dog Foods

Canned foods, dry foods and semi-moist foods are the three types of commercial dog foods you can choose from. Below explains how these differ from each other. This segment will help you choose what kind of food you want to provide for your pet.

Canned Foods

This food is also called "wet food". This offers higher moisture content as a can contains 75% to 80% of water. It has 2% to 15% of fat, and 8% to 15% of protein. Canned foods are easier to digest and contain low-energy nutrients. Your pet can eat more of this without gaining too much weight. Of all the types of dog foods, this has the highest cost per serving.

Dry Foods

Bags are where dry foods are packaged. To be practical, you need to buy a larger bag to save bigger amount of money. It contains 7% to 22% of fat, 18% to 40% of protein, 10% moisture, and 12% to 50% carbohydrates. This type of food contains high energy value.

It comes in different sizes, colour, and shapes as your dog can actually discern the shape, size, and texture of the food. The way the food feels is connected with its palatability, this food can stay fresh longer than those of the other food once it has been opened.

Semi - Moist Foods

Usually, these semi-moist foods are sold in boxes. It has 25% to 35% of carbohydrates, 15% to 25% of protein, 5% to 10% of fat, and 30% of water. Although this kind of food is more expensive than dry food, this is more palatable and easier to serve. If you are about to travel with your dog, this type of food is what you should bring. The downside of this food is that it contains corn syrup and sugar, ingredients which are high in sugar and can be harmful for dogs that have diabetes. Plus, it is said to have a high salt content as well.

Recommended Brands of Newfoundland Dog Foods

The quality of food is something you must consider as it is where the health of your dog relies on. You must be very wise in choosing the kind of food you are going to serve and what brand you should trust.

In order for you to maintain the proper nutrition of your dog, you will find below a list of the 5 best dog foods you may opt for your Newfoundland.

Nutro - Large Breed Adult Dog Food Formula

This dog food is manufactured by the Nutro Company who's known for the fresh and high-quality ingredients they use in producing their all-diet meals for both cats and dogs. This specific product is specially formulated for large breed dogs like Newfoundlands. The ingredients that make up this product are chicken meal, chicken, whole brown rice, rice bran, brewers rice, whole grain oatmeal, sunflower oil, chicken fat, and other various supplements. It contains chelated minerals that helps regulate and intensify nutrient absorption when chemically bonded to protein molecules. It is packed with chondroitin and glucosamine which strengthen joints and bones.

Orijen Large Breed Puppy Formula

This food is manufactured by a well-known company, Orijen pet food company, which produces high-quality diets for both dogs and cats. This product is specially formulated for large-breeds. This Orijen diet is made from regionally sourced ingredients namely fresh meats, cartilage, organs, fruits, vegetables ,boneless chicken, chicken liver, chicken meal, chicken fat, whole herring, turkey meal, boneless turkey, chicken liver oil, and whole eggs. It is an excellent source of fat, protein and digestible carbohydrates. This product is recommended for puppies as it is brimming with all the nutrients it needs for muscle growth and development.

Victor Yukon River Salmon & Sweet Potato Grain-Free Dry Dog Food

This formula is suitable for all Newfoundlands of different life stages namely puppies, adult,and lactating females. This product provides ample amount of nutrition as this ocean fish meal contains high levels of Omega 3 fatty acid along with Vitamin E which promotes glossy coat and healthy skin. It is made out of 32% of protein, 34% of carbohydrates, and 15% of fat. The good point about this product is that it is free from allergens like grain and gluten. The ingredients used for this product are Menhaden Fish Meal, Sweet Potato, Salmon, Peas, Canola Oil, Flax Seed, Dried Kelp Salt, Tomato Pomace, Yeast Culture, Dried Carrot and Dehydrated Alfalfa Meal.

Merrick Grain-Free Real Texas Beef + Sweet Potato Recipe Dry Dog Food

This product is manufactured by Merrick's Texas facility known for producing products made from locally-sourced ingredients. It caters an allergy-friendly nutrition as it is free from grains. It is made of Lamb Meal, Deboned Beef, Sweet Potatoes, Potatoes, Deboned Salmon, Blueberries, Salmon Oil, Pork Fat, Potato Protein, Organic Alfalfa, Apples, and Natural Flavor. This dry food will provide your dog a balanced nutrition as it is packed with lots of vitamins and minerals. It is formulated with Omega-3 and Omega 6 for a healthy skin and coat and with chondritin and glucosamine which improves mobility.

Now Fresh Grain-Free Breed Adult Recipe Dry Dog Food

This is manufactured by Now Fresh. This product is made from Potato, Peas, Deboned Turkey, Whole Dried Egg, Natural Flavour, Flaxseed, Canola Oil, Pea Fibre, Apples, Coconut Oil, Bananas, Blueberries, Cranberries, Pumpkin, Broccoli, Squash, Dried Kelp, Dried Chicory Root, Carrots, and Alfalfa. It is free from grains and gluten so you don't need to worry from these allergens.

Toxic Food for Dogs

Some foods that are edible and harmless for humans can be dangerous and fatal for dogs. It is must that you pose hazards for your pet as their metabolism is different from yours. Be careful and always take precautions on the food or snacks you administer to your Newfoundland. Being knowledgeable of this fact can help you save your dog from intoxication. We have below a list of common food items that may bring mild digestive upset and severe illness to your dog.

- Alcoholic beverages
- Apple seeds
- Apricot
- Avocado
- Bacon
- Bread Dough
- Chives
- Cherries
- Chocolates
- Citrus
- Coconut
- Coconut Oil
- Coffee
- Currants

- Dairy
- Fatty Trimmings
- Fruit pits
- Garlic
- Grapes
- Macadamia Nuts
- Mushrooms
- Onions
- Persimmon
- Potato leaves/stems
- Raisins
- Raw meat
- Rhubarb leaves
- Tomato leaves/stems

Chapter Six: Grooming and Training Your Newfoundlands

Everybody loves a good-looking and neat dog, thanks to proper grooming for making it possible. Other owners bring their dogs to luxurious grooming salons without knowing that they can actually groom their pets themselves without the need of spending huge amount of money. This can also be a great way for you and your dog to strengthen your bond. Training your pet is also one of the best bonding moment you and your pet might have. This breed is very trainable, but like any other dogs, you may expect their occasional naughtiness and stubbornness.

You really have to be patient especially if your dog cannot comprehend the command you're giving. This chapter will discuss points on how to groom your pet at home, along with the necessary tools you need in order to keep them pleasant-looking at all times. Newfoundlands are heavy shedders so this part is something you really have to take note of. Ways on how to properly train your Newfoundland without stressing your dog and yourself will be given as well.

How to Train Your Newfoundland

Newfoundlands are naturally smart and friendly giants. They grow up fast making proper training crucial for them. Training this breed at a very young age is a must as you want to avoid having a 125 pound dog that you cannot control. This breed is generally a willing worker and intelligent so expect that most of them will enjoy training sessions. This activity would benefit both you and your dog. Through it, you'll be able to build a stronger relationship with your pet in terms of mutual trust and respect. Good manners and confidence are just some of the values you'll be able to instil with your dog through training. Being able to teach and gain obedience from your dog will surely feel rewarding.

Remember that through your patience you'll be able to help your dog learn different life skills they need to know.

Daily Routines

The first thing you should teach your new puppy is the daily routines. The earlier the better! These should be the initial things your dog will get used to:

- **Where his food dish and water bowl is located** - make sure that these two will stay in one place
- **Where his bed is located**
- **When he will eat** - it is recommended for you to have established meal schedules daily in order for your dog to know when to expect his food.
- **What time will he get up**
- **Where he goes to urinate and defecate** - take your dog to the same place where he will do his thing. By this way, his scent will stimulate him to go

Your Dog's Name

Have your dog pay attention to you first. Let him know that you are calling him. Say his name whenever you are training, petting, and playing with him. By this you will establish in his mind that he is the one you are calling. If he responded quickly, give him praise.

Words

The most important words are "Good" and "No". These are praise and correction words your dog should learn. Training should be started as early as 2 to 3 months

Training Do's and Don'ts

- Do find a location with fewer distractions. This will allow your dog to have more focus on learning instead on something else.
- Don't forget to give rewards whenever your dog is in his most behave and obedient state. You can praise him so that he'll be able to associate the reward you have given to the command.
- Do plan sessions that will only last for 15 to 20 minutes. By this way you will stress your dog too much.
- Don't get frustrated if your dog doesn't follow your command. Do not raise your voice if your dog is being stubborn. Be patient and calm at all times.
- Don't feed your pet with a large meal before your training session, the more your dog wants the treat the more he'll follow your command.
- Do prepare the necessary equipment you need like the collar and the leash.

- Do end each session with a positive note.

Grooming Your Pet

Grooming a Newfoundland can be time consuming. It has a fluffy and thick coat that might easily accumulate dirt and debris. It has to be daily brushed to prevent mats and tangles from forming. This breed is "high maintenance" therefore you must really put a lot of effort for your dog. You don't have to bring your dog over expensive grooming salons. All you have to do is to follow these guidelines below:

- Use a large slicker brush to remove mats from your pet's hair. Brush his coat gently using slow and short downward strokes. If ever there is mat you have encountered, gently remove the tangle with the use of a de - tangler comb and if ever it can't be removed, use a pair of shears to carefully cut it out.
- Use a bristle brush or wire pin to go over the undercoat of your pet. Brush his undercoat by using gentle and short strokes opposite to the direction of his hair growth.
- Cut your dog's fur carefully. Remember it is better to cut less than too much.

- Trim the fur found on your dog's feet as it may accumulate bacteria and might cause infections. Be careful in trimming as you want to avoid them getting hurt.
- Give baths only when necessary. Too much bath can actually eliminate the natural oils on his coat. If dryness occurs, your dog might face skin problems. Giving your Newfoundland 2 baths per year is enough unless they have played in the dirt and if it is necessary to do so.
- Use lukewarm water in bathing your Newfoundland. Pour the water gently over his coat and give him a massage.
- If you are going to bathe your dog on a tub, put a non-slip mat for them stand on to prevent injuries.
- Put a thin line of specially formulated dog shampoo over your dog's back and gently massage it to distribute lather in able to thoroughly clean its body.
- Use a sprayer or shower to remove the residue from your dog's coat.
- Use a large clean towel in drying your dog. Make sure that he will not roam around the house with a wet fur or else dirt will easily accumulate on his skin.

How to Brush Your Dog's Teeth

Dental health is something you should not overlook. It is advisable that you brush your dog's teeth more often to prevent problems down the road. Here are the things you should do to keep your pet's teeth squeaky clean. Brushing your dog's teeth might be a little challenging. It might bring them an odd sensation. But don't feel disappointed if they refuse the first time you brush their teeth all you have to do is help them get used to it. Make sure that you are using the correct toothbrush and specially formulated toothpaste for dogs.

Introduce the taste of the toothpaste by putting a little amount of it on the tip of your finger and let your dog lick it. If the dog seems not to like it, you may opt to find another flavour that best suits your dog's preference. Brush your dog's teeth twice a week to prevent tartars from accumulating

How to Trim Your Dog's Nails

Most Newfoundlands are not fond of getting their feet and nails handled. Nail trimming and cutting may not be an activity they will enjoy but still it is necessary. Sometime dogs tend to have panic attacks when they see nail clippers so be sure to condition your dog to be calm before cutting their nails. In the process of it, hold their foot and cut small portion on the tips of their nails. Be mindful not to trim the pink part of the nails called "quick "as it supplies blood to the dog and it might cause bleeding. You can ask for your vet's assistance on how to properly trim your dog's nails without hurting them.

Cleaning Your Dog's Ears

The ears of dogs are prone to infection especially if not cleaned properly. In this case, you must be very careful in removing dirt from your pet's ears. There are many ear cleaners you can choose from in stores. It is advisable for you to buy a high-quality set of cleaners to ensure safety for your dog. Before cleaning your dog's ears, look for signs of infections first. If you dog's ear canals are red and inflamed, do not touch it and bring him immediately to the vet for a medical care. If not, you can proceed with this procedure. Hold upright the flap of the ear and gently clean the area using the tools you bought. After the procedure, give your dog a treat for being behaved and calm. You may ask for your vet's assistance as to how to clean your dog's ears properly.

Tips on How to Deal with Your Dog's Behavior

Just like any dogs, Newfoundlands may have other behaviour that shouldn't be tolerated as they have the potential to develop bad habits. But don't you worry. Instead of scolding them, stay calm for there are ways on how to manage these behaviours.

Chewing Objects

Chewing is said to remove their stress as well. If ever you saw your dog chewing inappropriate objects, you may want to give them toys on which they can chew on. Reward and give praise to your pet if he chose the appropriate item to chew

Excessive Barking

Barking may express fear, frustration, and anxiety. This is the most common bad behavior your dog might have. To end this unpleasant behavior, your dog should be able to learn words like "stop", "shush", and "quiet". If your dog stops barking after you said one of these words, give him a good pat in the head to reinforce the command

Begging at the table

No matter how cute and desperate they look, you should not give in to their begging. If you are going to eat, keep your dog busy with a chew toy but if the whining and barking continues, confine your dog away from the dinner table and let him out only if he is quiet.

Digging

Digging will always be a part of your dog's innate self as their ancestors have been doing this for a very long time. Instead of getting frustrated, try to understand that this is something they need to do in order to exercise their curiosity and relieve stress and boredom. We suggest that you give him his own digging spot, a sand box perhaps. Encourage him to dig only on his spot by burying something he will be interested at.

Chapter Seven: Showing Your Newfoundlands

Dog shows are one of the events that can really boost the dog lover in you. For a fact, Newfoundland breed is actually a patron to dog shows. Why not try to sign up for a dog competition? Your dog is very much eligible in this kind of event; for sure you'll have a great chance of bringing home the bacon. There are several kinds of dog shows you and your dog may enter. You should be first familiarized with it in order for you to know which kind best suits your dog.

Through this event both you and your pet will have a great time showing everyone your mutual respect and trust to each other. Plus, being part of such competition can help you discover other potentials of your dog. Through this chapter, you'll gain knowledge about the basics of dog shows, how you'll be able to prepare your dog on this activity, and what necessary paraphernalia you should bring. This will help you decide whether competitions like this is something you and your dog would like to take a shot.

Dog Shows

Dog shows have been held for quite a long time. This reveals not only the ability of the dog but also the skill of the handler. It plays a huge part in the development of your bond with your dog. In this segment, we're going to unravel the ways on how to find a show, how to fill up a form properly, which class to attend, etc.

- Finding a Show

There are lots of advertisements showing different dog shows around the world. Dog World and Our Dogs are the national dog papers on which you can see list of shows that will be held over the next two consecutive weeks.

You may also want to try to look for events over the internet. The first thing you have to do is to find a venue near you. Usually, these shows are held over sports center so that everyone can watch.

- Entering a Show

In entering a show, you must claim and fill-up the registration form. By this, you'll be able to verify if the show is regulated by the rules of the Kennel Club. If possible, you should have at least two copies of the form as they may be a need to do it again if ever you made corrections. Write as legibly as you can to avoid errors. Be ready for fees you may have to pay for registration.

- Choosing a Class

Check your schedule and find if there are available classes for Newfoundlands. If you have found a class, it is recommended for you to enter the breed class. Make sure you'll enter a class your dog is qualified in as for the reason that some has age requirements and other qualifications needed.

Standard for a Newfoundland

The standard is a criterion wherein the evaluation of your dog is being based. It helps judges, laymen, and breeders to know the essentials of the breed.

Head
- Massive with a broad skull
- The crown is arched
- Small and deep-set dark brown eyes free from irritation such as tearing
- Face and forehead are wrinkle-free
- Broad and deep muzzle
- Eyelids are closely fit without inversion
- Small and triangular ears with rounded tips
- Facial expression is soft and sweet

Dentition
- Teeth meet in level bite or scissor bite
- Dropped lower incisors

Coat
- Flat water-resistant double coat
- Outer coat is course and moderately full and long
- Undercoat is soft and dense

- Tail is full of long and dense hair
- Hair in the dace is fine and short, as well as in the muzzle

Gait
- Has strong drive
- Exceptional reach
- Smooth and rhythmic gait
- Hind legs and fore legs travel straight forward
- Moderate trot

Temperament
- Sweetness of temperament is the most important characteristics of Newfoundlands.

Grooming
- Neat and free from any mat
- Properly trimmed
- Whiskers need not to be trimmed

Preparations before the Competition

The idea of competing can be terrifying but if you have prepared yourself and your dog, this activity will just be a piece of cake. To ensure that your dog will do well in the competition, you should be able to condition him mentally and physically. Be mindful of the rules and regulations the show has set and make sure that you are able to comply with all of it and that your dog's pedigree is aligned with that of the show. Put all the necessary papers like medical certificates and license in a clear envelope for it might be needed.

Before attending to the event, you may want to visit other shows prior that of yours to familiarize yourself with the whole system. Pack your things inside a plastic box with a lid the day before the event. Make sure you have the following with you:

- Water bowl and water
- Collar and lead for the show
- Poo bags
- Money for the registration fee
- Pins for the entry number
- Treats for your dog
- Extra clothes
- Snacks
- Camera
- Grooming Kit
- Confirmation slip received at entry.
- Garbage bags

- Crate
- Crate Fan

If the event is held outdoors, bring the following:

- Folding chair
- Umbrella
- Sunglasses
- Plastic Mats

It is recommended for you to give your pet a bath the day before the actual show you won't be too tired on the day of the competition plus it will save you time. On the day of the competition, brush your dog's hair and make sure it's free from tangles and mat.

Things you should do at the event

When you are in the location, it is the best time for you to let your dog socialize with other pets. Be friendly at all times. Try to have good conversations with other handlers. By this way, you'll be able to share your thoughts and gain ideas on their experiences in taking care of their pet as well as in joining dog shows.

Senior handlers can be a little intimidating but you must be confident. The important thing is both you and your dog is doing your best and that both of you are enjoying. Do not be too anxious on what's going to happen. Just relax and seize the whole experience.

Chapter Eight: Breeding Basics

If you already miss having puppies playing around the house, maybe it's time for you to breed your Newfoundland. You need to learn the basics on how to breed them and how to take care of them during the whole process until the little ones come out. In this chapter, you'll be aware of what sexual dimorphism is, how the mating process happen, the things you should know about dog pregnancy, and the preparations you have to do before and after the delivery of the puppies.

What is Sexual Dimorphism?

Sexual Dimorphism denotes differences in the aspect of form between individuals of the opposite sex belonging in the same species. Dogs belong to the group of mammals and just like any mammals you'll be able to depict whether it is a male or female depending on its size, appearance, and of course their reproductive organs. In the case of Newfoundlands, males are bigger and heavier than the females. Looking at their body mass can help you decipher its sex without the need on looking at their sex organs.

Heat Cycle

Heat cycle or estrus cycle is the term used to denote the menstruation of female dogs. At the age of 9 to 12 months, females could already experience the cycle but this may vary. This happens once or twice every year. Unlike women, female dogs do not face menopausal as they age. Instead, they experience heat cycles throughout their lives.

There are four stages consisting the heat cycle:

- **Proestrus** - This may last for 4 to 20 days. In this stage, the females are still not willing to mate with a male dog. This is characterized with a vaginal discharge.

- **Estrus** - During this stage is where the point of mating occurs. It is defined by vaginal discharge and swollen vulva. This may go on for 5 to 13 days

- **Metestrus/Diestrus** - This stage happens after mating. This may last for 60 to 90 days. But if the female is pregnant, pregnancy may last for 60 to 64 days.

- **Anestrus** - This stage indicates the period of being inactive in both the hormonal and sexual aspects of the female between estrus phases. This may last for 2 to 3 months.

Steps to Know if Your Dog is Ready to Breed

There are signs that will indicate that your dog is ready for mating. You can follow the steps below in order to ensure that your female dog is ready to be bred.

- Check your dog's genital area. If her vulva is beginning to swell it means that she is experiencing heat. When you turn her, you should be able to see from behind her swollen vulva.

- Look if there are any discharges over your dog's bed or in your furniture. It may characterize blood or a milky pink or white discharge. Also, see to if it has a distinct smell since this is meant to catch the male's attention.

- Try to observe how often your dog urinates. If you're female dog urinates in small quantities but more frequently it means that she is in heat.

<u>Important Note:</u>

Do not push your dog too hard in this process of breeding in order not to put your dog under too much stress. You may ask for your vet's assistance to make sure that you catch your dog's peak during her fertile period for a bigger chance of getting pregnant.

Signs of Canine Pregnancy

These signs might indicate that your female dog is pregnant but still it is best for you to consult your veterinarian to avoid false hopes.

- Loss of appetite
- Increase vaginal discharge
- Decrease in level of activity and energy
- Enlargement of the abdomen
- Enlargement of nipples

Dog Pregnancy

Gestation

Gestation is a term to coin pregnancy. Generally, the gestation period for Newfoundlands last approximately for 63 to 65 days from the day of conception, but this may vary as conception is often hard to predict. Dog pregnancy last shorter than humans, about 9 weeks in total. In this period, make sure that your pregnant dog gets all the nutrients she need. You may seek for your veterinarian's professional advice in order to take the right steps in taking care of your expecting pet.

Labor and Delivery

After the end of the gestation period, labor begins. There are three stages of labor.

Stage One

This happens during the first 12 to 24 hours of labor. Muscular contractions in the uterus increase in this stage although these are still not visible. The symptoms your dog is in labor are panting, change in behavior, restlessness, loss of appetite, clear vaginal discharge, and vomiting.

Stage Two

In this stage, puppies are delivered. This can last for 1 to 24 hours. A female dog will deliver one puppy at a time in the intervals that should not last more than 1 to 2 hours so it will be advisable for you to know how many puppies you are expecting. You may seek for your veterinarian's help during delivery.

Stage Three

The placenta is the one being delivered in this stage. This happens shortly after the two stages occurred.

Litter

Usually, Newfoundlands can deliver 4 to 12 dogs. But this may vary. It is advisable for you to know how many puppies your dog is going to deliver. Ultrasound is the most common way to know the number of puppies you should expect.

Maturity

Growth spurts happen in this breed. Newfoundland puppies mature when they reach 2 years of age unlike other breeds that only takes a year to mature. Be sure to make each and every moment count while they are still in their cute little pup self, as growing up is another phase you have to deal with.

Pseudo - pregnancy

Although your dog might possess the symptoms of being pregnant, it is still the best to consult your veterinarian since there is a condition called Pseudo-pregnancy on which your dog might be experiencing signs of pregnancy although they aren't really pregnant. This is also called "false pregnancy". The symptoms it shows are vomiting, loss of appetite, abdominal distension, restlessness, behavioral changes, and increase in the size of the mammary glands.

Multiple Fathers

Although very rare, dogs can actually be impregnated by more than one dog. During breeding, if your female dog mates with more than one male dog within the span of 7 days during the heat cycle, there is a chance that the litter she will be delivering might have different fathers.

Tips in Raising Puppies

Puppies need special attention as they are young and in need of your tender loving care. It might be challenging as they require more attention than the adults. Below are some tips you may use in order to raise a puppy well.

- As soon as the puppies arrive, bring them to the vet as soon as possible. It will be better if they'll have their first health check-up immediately to ensure that they are in the best condition. A sick pup no matter how minor the illness will be might not be able to adjust well with the new environment he belongs to.

- Let the puppies be crate trained. As much as possible, make this as a positive experience for them. Let them know where their safe space is located. Provide them the most comfortable crate they will ever have. Place the crate near their mother so that they will be able to bond with them and for the reason that she needs to feed them through her mammary glands.

- Ensure that the puppies get plenty of rest. Puppies, just like babies, need lots of sleep in order to grow. Let them rest in a quiet area in your home. Do not bother them when they are in their quiet time.

- Make sure that the puppies meet their nutritional needs as it is vital for their growth and development. You may ask for your vet's recommendation as to what kind of food your puppies should eat and if there's a need for them to take vitamins.

- Socialize your pet in order for them to become well-behaved adult in the future. Spend lots of time with them. Expose them with other animals and to other people as well.

Chapter Nine: Common Diseases and Health Requirements

Many breeds are prone to serious health conditions. Unfortunately, Newfoundlands are one of them but there's nothing to worry about. With proper learning you'll be able to prevent these diseases from coming. Knowing the health condition and the most common health problems Newfoundland will give you ideas what precautions to take in order to avoid the development of such diseases. Health is something you must not overlook.

The information you'll get from this chapter will surely be of great help for you. We'll help you be familiarized with the different disorders and diseases your dog might potentially carry as well as how to strengthen your dog's immune system through series of vaccinations.

Common Health Problems

Through this section, you'll be able to discover some of the most common diseases Newfoundlands have. Being knowledgeable about these will give you a head start against its development as there are remedies you may take in order to prevent these from arising. If ever these have already affected your dog, there are ways to treat each and every disease.

Just like any other breed, Newfoundlands are prone on having orthopedic disorders, congenital heart diseases, non-congenital heart diseases, optical diseases, and other common illness. Monitoring your dog's health is always a must. Be sure that you and your vet have a common understanding with regards to the health of your pet.

Eye Problems

- **Ectropion** - This is also called as "Lower Eyelid Droop." This eye condition is characterized by the outward rolling of the eyelid exposing the part of tissue lining the inner lids. This problem can result to a serious corneal disease that can rob your dog's eyesight. The signs indicating ectropion are conjunctiva inflammation, lower eyelid protrusion, and facial staining of tears caused by malfunctioning tear ducts.

- **Cataracts** - This is characterized by cloudiness in the lens of the dog's eyes which opacity varies from partial to complete.When the lenses are clouded, the light passing to the retina is being blocked. This may actually result to a loss of vision. Cataracts are caused by old age, diabetes mellitus, radiation exposure, and electric shock.

Circulatory System Diseases

Congenital

- **Subaortic Stenosis (SAS)** - This condition is developed when the aortic valve in the heart is being covered with a ring of tissue causing the blood flow to curb increasing the amount of pressure in the heart. This disease is considered as a complex genetic disorder. Puppies that belong in a large breed are usually the ones affected by this congenital disease.

It is advisable for you to let your vet check your puppy's heart as this condition can be very fatal for your pet.

- **Pulmonic Stenosis -** This heart defect refers to an obstruction found in the right ventricular outflow concerning the pulmonary artery and the right ventricle. In this condition, there is a narrowing during ventricular contraction causing muscle thickening in the heart.

- **Tricuspid Valve Dysplasia (TVD)** - This heart ailment is characterized by malformations in the chordae tendineae, tricuspid valve leaflets, and papillary muscles resulting to a blood leak from the right ventricle following the right atrium.

Non – Congenital

- **Dilated Cardiomyopathy (DCM) -** This develops in the later stages of a dog's life. This is defined by the thinning of the muscles found in the heart leaving the dog with a malfunctioning enlarged heart. Symptoms include shortness of breath, anorexia, shortness of breath, loss of consciousness, abdominal distension, and lethargy.

Orthopedic Disorders

- **Elbow Anomaly** - This kind of orthopedic disorder in Newfoundlands have only been discovered lately and still under the process of research headed by The Newfoundland Club of America. This condition is characterized with the dislocation of the bones found in the front logs of this breed. Heredity is being considered as the cost of it. In as early as four weeks, a dog can be diagnosed with Elbow Anomaly.

- **Panosteitis** - This disease is often characterized by lameness and limpness which may last from 2 to 3 weeks and may rotate from one leg to another. It is where the long bones of the dog is affected with inflammation. The cause of it is currently unknown but genetics and infection are suspected to may have caused this type of orthopedic disorder. Generally, dogs with the age of 5 to 18 months are the ones being affected by it. The signs indicating panosteitis are weight loss, depression, anorexia, and fever.

- **Hip Dysplasia -** This disorder is one of the most common orthopaedic disorders for dogs. The development of this skeletal disease is being traced with genetic and environmental factors like genes for having a loose hip, nutrition, mass of the pelvic muscle, and obesity. It is a condition wherein the hip joints failed to develop normally and is deteriorating gradually as time goes by. Large breeds are often affected by this. As early as four months of age, this disorder might already develop. If ever you'll notice signs of joint looseness, pain in hip joints, difficulty in rising, decrease in muscle mass in thigh muscles, and decreased range of activity, you should immediately consult your vet.

- **Ruptured Cruciate Ligament -** The major part of dog's knee is called "cruciate ligament". A sudden injury or rupture in the ligament may cause lameness. Genetics are said to be a large contributor in this kind of illness. Middle age dogs are the ones who commonly suffer from it.

- **Elbow Dysplasia -** This condition happens whenever there is an abnormal growth of tissue, bone, or cell. Elbow dysplasia is defined by the degeneration and malformation of the joint found in the elbow.

This may cause forelimb lameness and elbow pain. Dogs in the age of 4 to 18 months are usually the ones being diagnosed with it. Males are more likely to be affected with this illness rather than the females. Symptoms of having elbow dysplasia are decreased range of motion, accumulation of fluid in the joint and persistent elbow and forelimb lameness.

Skin Diseases

- **Pyotraumatic dermatitis (Hot Spots) -** Also known as acute moist dermatitis, it is one of the most familiar skin condition of Newfoundlands. This skin condition can spread promptly so you must be able to attend to this skin disease immediately. Factors that cause this skin problem are allergies, parasites, bacterial infections, and hot weather.

Other Health Problems

- **Hyperthyroidism** - This refers to the inadequate production of thyroid hormone. Poor coat, lethargy, and weight gain are some of its symptoms. Middle age dogs and older dogs are the ones being affected by this condition.

- **Bloat** - Also known as gastric dilatation volvulus, bloat is a condition that can be very fatal for dogs. This is characterized by the expansion of the stomach as it is filled with gas, fluid, or food. For this reason, the organs experience too much pressure; this may cause curbing of the blood flow to the heart and stomach lining, problems in breathing, and tearing of the stomach wall.

Immunizations

Immunizations or vaccinations are a must in the sense of public health as it prevents dogs from catching diseases as well as the risk of spreading communicable illnesses. No matter how healthy your dog is, it is still necessary for you to provide him with all the vaccinations he needed. Puppies between the ages of 7 to 8 weeks are recommended to be immunized. Usually, breeders give initial vaccinations before letting the puppy be taken by the new owner. Be sure to ask your breeder about this matter.

The recommended vaccinations for Newfoundlands are divided into 2 categories. Core vaccines are usually administered to every dog breed, while non-core vaccines are only recommended for certain types of dogs.

The immunization needed by this breed include the following:

Core Vaccines
- Canine Rabies
- Canine hepatitis
- Canine parovirus
- Canine Distemper or Hard Pad

Non-core Vaccines
- Kennel Cough
- Leptospirosis
- Canine Parainfluenza

Vaccination Schedule for Newfoundlands

Below is a possible vaccination schedule for your Newfoundland but it is advisable that you ask for your veterinarian's recommendation regarding the vaccination of your pet in order to ensure the protection of your pet.

5 weeks old

During this age, your dog is at a high risk of catching parvovirus. This is usually the time veterinarians administer parvo shots.

12 weeks old and above

This is the time wherein a vaccination for canine rabies will be given. Age requirement for rabies shot may vary according to the law that prevails in your area.

12 weeks to 15 weeks old

Combination vaccine can be given to dogs at this age. This may include leptospirosis, canine parainfluenza, kennel cough, and canine distemper.

Chapter Ten: Care Sheet and Summary

You've reached the last chapter of this book. You've come so far and we hope that you have learned so much. We are so excited on the journey you and your pet will have. We hope that your learning doesn't stop here. You can try to make your own research at home to further intensify your learning on how to become a responsible owner.

This is the last but definitely not the least chapter. In this section of the book, we will give you a synopsis of all the important points discussed in the prior chapters so that if ever you want to check out a topic, there's no need for you to read the whole book but instead a quick glance will do.

Biological Information

Taxonomy: Kingdom Animalia, Phylum Chordata, Class Mammalia, Order Carnivora, Family Canidae, Genus Canis, and Species Lupus Familiaris
Country of Origin: Canada
Breed Size: large breed
Body Type and Appearance: It has a massive and powerful body structure.
Height: a male Newfoundland stand 26 to 28 inches and females stand in an average of 26 inches tall
Weight: male has a general weight of 130 to 150 pounds; 100 to 120 pounds for females
Coat Length: long and straight without curl
Coat Texture: soft and desnse
Color: Black, black and white, brown, gray and may come with white markings
Other name: Newfie, Newf

Newfoundlands as Pets

Temperament: sweet, friendly, and gentle
Other pets: can go well with other especially if socialized at a young age

Major Pro: can easily get along with others especially kids

Major Con: heavy shedders

Legal Requirements and Dog Licensing:

United States: There are no federal requirements for licensing either cats or even dogs. It is regulated only at the state level.

United Kingdom: Licensing for dogs is mandatory and there will be a need to get a special permit if you plan to travel with your dog into or out of the country.

Russia: Licensing is mandatory. Micro-chipping is strictly implemented.

Other countries: Usually documents such as your state permit for your dog, current health condition, and rabies or vaccinations certificate are needed.

Purchasing and Selecting a Healthy Breed

Where to Purchase: Pet Stores, Private Breeders, Online Stores, Dog Conventions

Characteristics of a Reputable Breeder: One sign that the breeder you are having a conversation with is accountable if he asks questions about yourself too. It means that they are making sure that the dog or dogs he own will be transferred in good hands and will be well-taken care of.

Characteristics of a Healthy Breed: The dog should be free from any illness, infections, injuries, and abnormality in their body structure. It should be playful, can socialize well with humans and other animals without shying away, and active.

Habitat Requirements for Newfoundlands: This breed is a large one and is need of a spacious place to stay and rest. Every dog needs a place to call their own and therefore you must respect their territory and space.

Housing Temperature: Newfoundlands should be kept in a cold to temperate weather. If it is summer time it is recommended that you let your dog indoors as much as possible as they may catch heat stroke easily. You may have the need to provide your dog air coolers or electric fans whenever the weather is too hot for them.

Nutrition and Food

Recommended Brands of Newfoundland Foods: Nutro Large Breed Adult Dog Food Formula, Orijen Large Breed Puppy Formula, Victor Yukon River Salmon & Sweet Potato Grain-Free Dry Dog Food, Merrick Grain-Free Real Texas Beef + Sweet Potato Recipe Dry Dog Food, Now Fresh Grain-Free Breed Adult Recipe Dry Dog Food

How to Feed Your Newfoundland: Establish meal schedule for your dog for him to know when to expect his meals. Be careful not to overfeed your dog as it may cause obesity. Read and follow the feeding instructions found on the packaging of the dog food you bought.

Feeding Amount/Frequency: The frequency in how often you should feed your dog should be based on its size, age, weight, and activity level. If your dog is more active, it requires more energy from food. It is advisable that your dog intakes the amount of food 2-3% of its body weight per day.

Grooming and Training Your Newfoundlands

How to Brush Your Dog's Teeth: Brush your dog's teeth twice a week to avoid tartar accumulation
How to Trim Your Dog's Nails: Once a week or twice a month will be enough.
Cleaning Your Dog's Ears: Using high-quality cleaning tools, remove the dirt from your dog's ears carefully. Check for any signs of infection before doing so.

Showing Your Newfoundlands

Criteria for Judging
- Head
- Dentition
- Coat
- Gait
- Temperament
- Grooming

Breeding Your Newfoundlands

Gestation Period: 63 days from the time of conception

Litter Size: Female Newfoundlands usually give birth to four to nine puppies, but this may vary

Maturity: Puppies mature when they reach 2 years of age

Common Diseases and Health Requirements

- **Eye Problems -** Ectropion, Cataract
- **Circulatory System Diseases -** (Congenital) Subaortic Stenosis (SAS), Pulmonic Stenosis, Tricuspid Valve Dysplasia (TVD); (Non- Congenital) Dilated Cardiomyopathy
- **Orthopedic Disorders -** Elbow Anomaly, Panosteitis, Hip Dysplasia, Ruptured Cruciate Ligament, Elbow Dysplasia

- **Skin Diseases -** Pyrotraumatic Dermatitis (Hot Spots)
- **Other Health Problems -** Hyperthyroidism, Bloat

Recommended Vaccinations:

Core Vaccines
- Canine Rabies
- Canine hepatitis
- Canine parovirus
- Canine Distemper or Hard Pad

Non-core Vaccines
- Kennel Cough
- Leptospirosis
- Canine Parainfluenza

Glossary of Dog Terms

Abdomen: Known as the belly

Acetabulum: Portion of the sacrum that is concave

Achondroplasia: Genetic dwarfism caused by an abnormal development of cartilage found at the ends of the long bones

Action: Shown by functions of locomotion

Acquired Immunity: Immunity made possible through the development of antibodies or injection of antiserum.

Agent: Another term used for handler

Agility Trials: Competition that has been organized at which dogs undergo a series of obstacles and jumps in three classes

Albino: Rare genetic condition which results to white hair

All-Breed Show: A conformation show where all AKC-recognized breeds are exhibited.

Almond Eyes: Shape of the eyes that are elongated rather than rounded

American Kennel Club: It is an organization established in line with the laws of the State of New York for purebred dog's events whose are all about adopting and enforcing uniform rules and regulations in shows.

Apple Head: A skull with a round shape

Articulation: It happens when two bones meet

Babbler: A tongue-giving hound when not on the trail

Bad Mouth: Characterized by crooked teeth

Bait: Used to catch a dog's attention

Barrel Hocks: Known as spread hocks, a type of hocks that turn out which causes the feet to toe in.

Barring: Markings that are stripes

Beady: Used to describe small, round, and glittering eyes.

Beard: The long hair growing on the under jaw.

Brock: A badger

C.A.R: Companion Animal Recovery

C.G.C: Canine Good Citizen

Camel Back: Back that is arched

Carpals: Bones found in the wrist

Clip: A method of coat trimming

Collar: A material where the leash is attached and is used to restrain a dog. Usually made from materials like chain, nylon or leather.

Colitis: A type of inflammation found in the colon.

Dam: A parent who's female

Date of Whelping: Other term for date of birth

Digit: It means toe

Dermatitis: A kind of inflammation in the skin.

Distemper: A highly infectious disease often characterized by a fever, discharge from the eyes and nose, vomiting, partial paralysis, and loss of appetite.

Dog Fancy: Used to coin a group of people who are actively and expressly interested in the promotion of purebred dogs.

Dog Show: Also known as conformation show. It is where dogs are judged on how well they met their own breed standards

Ears: An organ used for the sense of hearing

Enteritis: A type of inflammation in the intestinal tract

Entropion: A genetic condition which results in the turning in of the eyelid and causes corneal ulceration.

Even Bite: Also called the level bite wherein the meeting of upper and lower incisors is exact.

Feathering: Term used to denote the long fringe of hair found on the ears, legs,tail, or body.

Flying Ears: It is defined by drop ears and semi-pricked ears that can fly or stand

FRP: Failure to receive papers

FSS ®: Foundation Stock Service ®

Gait: It is the pattern of footsteps or walk in general at various rates of speed

Game: Birds or any animal being hunted

Gaskin: Lower thigh

Groom: Keeping the neatness of a dog by through brushing, combing, or trimming

Groups: Breed groups that the AKC has made; herding, hound, working, toy, sporting, terrier, and non-sporting.

Hallmark: Characteristic that's distinguished

Haunch Bones: Hip Bones

Hip Dysplasia: Abnormality in the hip bones

Hormone: A peptide or steroid which may be responsible growth or metabolism.

Humane Societies: Groups which are advocating against animal and human abuse

Hypothermia: A term used to coin a condition wherein the body is experiencing a very cold environment resulting to an abnormally low body temperature

Impure Breeding: Crossbred

In Whelp: It means pregnant

Inbreeding: It is the mating of two dogs of the same breed.

Iris: A colored membrane part of the eye neighboring the pupil.

Jacobson's Organ: A sense organ found in the roof of the dog's mouths.

Jowls: Flesh of the jaws and lips

Kennel: An building that is enclosed and where dogs are being kept

Kennel Cough: Also known as Tracheobronchitis of dogs

Kennel Name: Registered Name; prefix

Kink Tail: It is characterized by a deformity in the caudal vertebrae resulting to tail that's bent.

Knuckling Over: A condition wherein the wrist joint is faulty structured allowing it to flex forward under the standing dog's weight.

Lame: Irregularity of locomotion

Leather: It denotes the flap of the ear

Legal Ownership: The type of ownership which is governed by the law's rules

Leptospirosis: A kind of disease that is infectious to domestic animals.

Lien: The right to hold and sell property of a debtor

Litter Application: Used for litter registration

Lumbering: Gait characterized with awkwardness

Luxation: Anatomical structure's dislocation

Mad Dog: A dog that has turned rabid

Mandible: Bone found in the lower jaw

Mask: A dark shading found in the fore face

Maternal Immunity: A temporary immunity that can be passed from a mother to her offspring while inside the uterus.

Microchip: A device implanted underneath the skin of your dog for licensing

Molera: Skull's incomplete ossification

National Specialty: These are events that have been hosted by the parent club

Natural Breed: It happens when a breed of dog occurred naturally even without the need for a process of selective breeding.

Neuter: The process of spaying or castrating

Nick: A type of breeding that has a tendency to produce desirable puppies.

Nictitating Membrane: The third eyelid; It is the transparent inner eyelids of some birds, mammals, and reptiles.

Occiput: Skull's posterior point

Obedience Trial: This is an event which an obedience degree can be merited; this is in line with the rules of AKC

Obesity: It is a condition referring to an excessive accumulation of fat leading to the condition of being overweight or obese.

Omnivore: An animal or person that eats both vegetable and meat of animals.

Ovulate: The process of ova production; the discharging of eggs from the ovary

Parvovirus: A common disease of canines that is highly contagious and fatal.

Pedigree: A written record of a dog's genealogy which includes three generations or more.

Pelvis: Hip Bones

Phenotype: An observable physical or biochemical characteristics of an organism determined by genetic makeup and environmental influences.

Quarantine: An restriction of free movement or enforced isolation imposed in order to prevent the spread of any contagious disease

Quick: A vein that runs through a dog's nails or claw; it where blood is supplied

Racy: Tall Built

Registries: These are used to denote the organizations responsible for keeping the official dog records on specific subjects

Reward: It is something used as a motivating factor to stimulate desired behavior. It is often characterized by treats and praises.

Saddle: These are the markings in the shape of a saddle that can be found on the back with various color definitions

Scent: It is the odor left by a bird or any animal in trail

Seeing eye dog: A dog specially trained to assist blind persons

Shock: A physiological reaction caused by severe emotional or physical trauma.

Show Quality: A kind of dog pedigreed to meet the official breed standard in order to become fit to compete in dog shows

Show Hours: Event hours

Topical: A type of drug that can be applied on a localized surface of the body

Topline: The outline of the dog from behind the withers up to the tail

Trail: Hunting through smelling the scent of the ground

Trim: One process of grooming the coat

Ulna: One of the bones found in the ulna

Undercoat: A soft and dense short coat lying underneath a longer top coat.

Underline: A combination of contours of both the brisket and the abdominal floor.

Utility Dog (UD): A title awarded to a dog by the AKC as a in line with his winnings towards certain minimum scores in utility classes

Vaccine: An administered shot for the preparation towards killed or weakened pathogen, usually a bacterium or virus, in order to avoid diseases.

Vent: An opening to the anus

Walk: It is the dog's gaiting pattern wherein three legs are supporting the body at all times on which each foot are lifting on the ground in a regular sequence one at a time.

Wind: Being able to catch the scent of game.

Winging: A gaiting fault on which one or both front feet twist outward while the limbs are swinging in a forward manner.

Wirehair: A hard coat with a wiry texture

Xiphoid Process: The sternum's cartilage process

Zoonosis: Used to coin certain disease of animals that can be easily transmitted to humans like rabies.

Zygomatic Arch: A bony ridge extending posteriorly from under the eye orbit.

Index

E

F

G

H

Photo Credits

Page 1 Photo by user Marcia O 'Connoe via Flickr.com, https://www.flickr.com/photos/97477873@N00/19072755366

Page 3 Photo by user Bearskin Lodge via Flickr.com, https://www.flickr.com/photos/bearskinlodge/8064992403

Page 10 Photo by userMatty Sides via Flickr.com, https://www.flickr.com/photos/mattsidesinger/5601644869/

Page 24 Photo by userlaura jess via Flickr.com, https://www.flickr.com/photos/laurajess/

Page 38 Photo by user Matty Sides via Flickr.com, https://www.flickr.com/photos/mattsidesinger/5372059493/

Page 45 Photo by user Matty Sides via Flickr.com, https://www.flickr.com/photos/mattsidesinger/7790384598/

Page 58 Photo by user Matty Sides via Flickr.com, https://www.flickr.com/photos/mattsidesinger/6062566339/

Page 68 Photo by userMatty Sides via Flickr.com, https://www.flickr.com/photos/mattsidesinger/5372660840/

References

"All You Need To Know About Dog Mating"
Pethelpful.com
< https://pethelpful.com/dogs/Dog-Mating>

"A Dog's Menstrual (Heat) Cycle" Petwave.com
<https://www.petwave.com/dogs/basics/breeding/heat/aspx
>

"Breed History of Newfoundlands"
Newfounlandpuppies.org
<http://www.newfoundlandpuppies.org/breedhistory.html>

"Bringing Pets To Russia" Pettravel.com
<http://www.pettravel.com/immigration/russia.cfm>

"Cataracts in Dogs" Petmd.com
< http://www.petmd.com/dog/conditions/eye/c_dg_cataract>

"Common Health Problems in Newfoundlands"
Capricciofarmnewfs,com
<http://www.capricciofarmnewfs,com/health.htm

"Considerations" Newfoundlandpuppies.org
<http://www.newfoundlandpuppies.org/considerations.html
>

"Cost of Owning A Dog" Wallethub.com
<https://wallethub.com/edu/cost-of-owning-a-dog/15563/>

"Dog Food for Newfoundlands" Dogfoodguru.guru
<http://dogfood.guru/newfoundland/>

"Dog Licensing and Microchipping" Nidirect.gov.uk
< https://www.nidirect.gov.uk/articles/dog-licensing-and-microchipping>

"Dog- Proofing Your Home" Thebark.com
<http://thebark.com/content/dog-proofing-your-home-room-room-guide?page=2>

"Foods That Are Bad For Dogs" Dogtime.com
< http://dogtime.com/dog-health/general/5504-bad-foods-for-dogs-list>

"Fruits & Vegetables That Are Toxic to Dogs"
Iheartdogs.com
< https://iheartdogs.com/10-fruits-vegetables-that-are-toxic-to-dogs/3/>

"Getting Ready" Ncanewfs.com
<http://www.ncanewfs.org/newfs/pages/Gettingready.html>

"Glossary" Akc.org
<http://www.akc.org/about/glossary>

"History of the Newfoundlands" Retrieverman.net
<https://retrieverman.net/2012/04/20/teasing-apart-the-history-of-the-newfoundland-dog-the-st-johns-water-dog-and-the-retrievers/>

"How to Feed a Dog" Wikihow.pet
< http://www.wikihow.pet/Feed-a-Dog>

"How to Help Your Dog Whelp or Deliver Puppies"
Wikihow.com
<http://www.wikihow.com/Help-Your-Dog-Whelp-or-Deliver-Puppies>

"How to Train a Dog" Wikihow.com
< http://www.wikihow.com/Train-a-Dog>

"Newfoundlands" Dogs-and-dog-advice.com
<http://www.dogs-and-dog-advice.com/newfoundland_dog>

"Newfoundlands" Justdogbreeds.com
<https://www.justdogbreeds.com/newfoundland.html>

"Newfoundlands" Makennels.com
<http://www.makkennels.com/newfoundland.html>

"Newfoundlands" Petmd.com
<http://www.petmd.com/dog/breeds/c_dg_newfoundland>

"Newfoundland Dog Health Issues" Gentle-newfoundland-dogs.com
<https://www.gentle-newfoundland-dogs.com/newfoundland-dog-health.html>

"People Foods That Can Be Dangerous to Dogs" Dogfoodadvisor.com
< https://www.dogfoodadvisor.com/people-foods-dangerous-dogs/>

"Pet Shop Puppies" Yourpurebredpuppy.com
<http://www.yourpurebredpuppy.com/buying/articles/petshops-and-pet-stores.html>

"Steel Dog Bowls" Walmart.com
<https://www.walmart.com/c/ep/steel-dog-bowls>

"Showing Your Newfoundlands" Northernnewfoundlandclub.org.uk
<http://www.northernnewfoundlandclub.org.uk/showing1.html

"Temperament of Newfoundlands" Dogtemperament.com
<http://www.dogtemperament.com/newfoundland-
temperament/#>

"Tips for Dog Proofing Your Home" Rover.com
< https://www.rover.com/dog-proofing-your-home/>

" Tips for Showing Your Dog" Dogs.lovetoknow.com
< http://dogs.lovetoknow.com/dog-information/ten-tips-
showing-your-dog>

"The Cost of Dog Ownership" Thespruce.com
< https://www.thespruce.com/the-cost-of-dog-ownership-
1117321>

"Vaccination Schedules for Dogs and Puppies"
Peteducation.com
<https://www.peteducation.com/article.cfm?c=2+2115&aid=9
50>

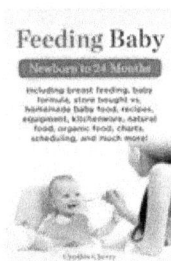

Feeding Baby
Cynthia Cherry
978-1941070000

Axolotl
Lolly Brown
978-0989658430

Dysautonomia, POTS
Syndrome
Frederick Earlstein
978-0989658485

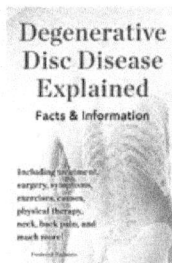

Degenerative Disc
Disease Explained
Frederick Earlstein
978-0989658485

Sinusitis, Hay Fever,
Allergic Rhinitis Explained
Frederick Earlstein
978-1941070024

Wicca
Riley Star
978-1941070130

Zombie Apocalypse
Rex Cutty
978-1941070154

Capybara
Lolly Brown
978-1941070062

Eels As Pets
Lolly Brown
978-1941070167

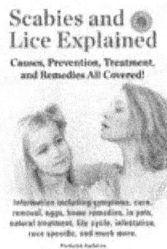

Scabies and Lice Explained
Frederick Earlstein
978-1941070017

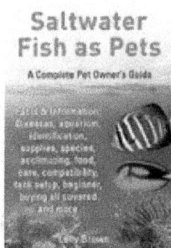

Saltwater Fish As Pets
Lolly Brown
978-0989658461

Torticollis Explained
Frederick Earlstein
978-1941070055

Kennel Cough
Lolly Brown
978-0989658409

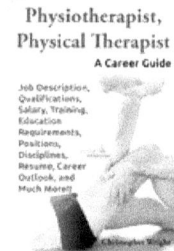

Physiotherapist, Physical
Therapist
Christopher Wright
978-0989658492

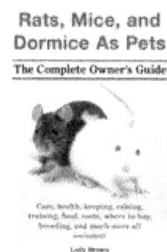

Rats, Mice, and Dormice
As Pets
Lolly Brown
978-1941070079

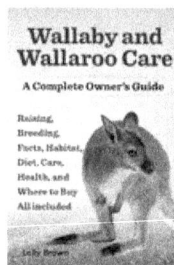

Wallaby and Wallaroo Care
Lolly Brown
978-1941070031

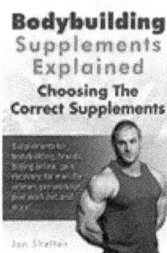

Bodybuilding Supplements
Explained
Jon Shelton
978-1941070239

Demonology
Riley Star
978-19401070314

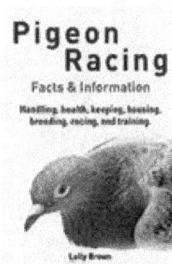

Pigeon Racing
Lolly Brown
978-1941070307

Dwarf Hamster
Lolly Brown
978-1941070390

Cryptozoology
Rex Cutty
978-1941070406

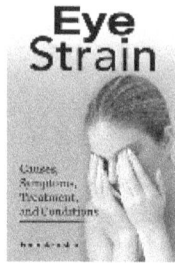

Eye Strain
Frederick Earlstein
978-1941070369

Inez The Miniature Elephant
Asher Ray
978-1941070353

Vampire Apocalypse
Rex Cutty
978-1941070321

www.ingramcontent.com/pod-product-compliance
Lightning Source LLC
LaVergne TN
LVHW051642080426
835511LV00016B/2446